AMONG US

PLAYBOOK

Among Us: 100% Unofficial Game Guide
Copyright © 2021 by Egmont Books UK Limited
All in-game images © 2021 by Innersloth LLC
Designed by Grant Kempster

ISBN 978-0-06-313582-6

21 22 23 24 25 RTLO 10 9 8 7 6 5 4 3 2

❖

First US edition, 2021
Originally published in 2021 in Great Britain by 100% Unofficial,
part of Egmont Books UK Limited, an imprint of HarperCollins Publishers.

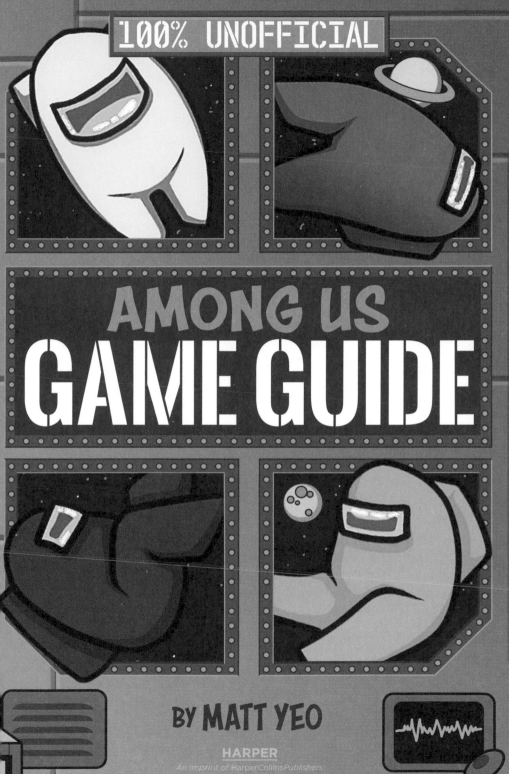

100% UNOFFICIAL

AMONG US
GAME GUIDE

BY MATT YEO

HARPER
An imprint of HarperCollinsPublishers

CONTENTS

INTRODUCTION

Initially a sleeper hit when it launched in 2018, Among Us from developer Innersloth went on to become a massive success and one of the most popular video games of 2020. A multiplayer murder mystery set in a variety of futuristic levels, Among Us casts players in the roles of anonymous spacesuit-wearing characters in a super-tense whodunit experience.

In *Among Us: 100% Unofficial Game Guide*, you'll find the best hints, tips, and tricks for surviving as a Crewmate and learn how to work out which players are actually sneaky alien shapeshifters. You'll also discover advanced strategies for being an Impostor, including the best ways to get rid of other players without being discovered and how to successfully sabotage levels.

Among Us: 100% Unofficial Game Guide takes you from the flight deck of The Skeld and the atmospheric heights of MIRA HQ to the strange landscape of Polus, and is guaranteed to help you impress your friends with your gaming skills to become . . . the ultimate survivor!

How to Play

Looking for a great multiplayer game to try with your friends? Then Among Us is just what you're after! It's available on PC, mobile devices and the Nintendo Switch and is due to hit more consoles soon. Take a look at this guide to find out where you can play, as well as how to get started.

Know Your Role

Players take on the roles of either Crewmates or Impostors in a tense game of sci-fi murder mystery. Play as a Crewmate and work together to find out which one of you is an alien Impostor, or become the Impostor and try to sabotage the level.

Multiplayer Mayhem

Up to 10 players can join Local or Online matches, allowing you to team up with your mates to survive. Each game takes place on one of three space-bound maps. Each map has a variety of rooms within it, which contain items to use, tasks to complete and areas to sabotage.

PC Controls

Gamers using a PC to play Among Us can use a combination of keyboard and mouse controls:

Spacebar or E – Use keys
Escape – Close open menu
Tab – Map
Q – Kill nearby Crewmate if you're an Impostor
R – Report dead body
W – Up

A – Left
S – Down
D – Right
Arrow Keys – Move
Alt + Enter – Toggle screen size
Left Mouse Button – Mini games and menus

Touchscreen Controls

Players can choose "Joystick" from the settings menu to move around with the virtual thumbstick in the bottom left of the screen and tap "Use" to activate items. With the "Touch" option selected, press your finger on the screen to move your character. Tap on any highlighted item to use it.

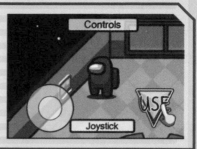

Playing As A Crewmate

To win the game as a Crewmate, you'll all have to work together to complete a set number of special tasks. You'll also need to keep an eye out for suspicious activity, report any sabotage, call Emergency Meetings, and try to work out which of you is an Impostor.

Playing As An Impostor

Take on the role of an Impostor and you have to sabotage levels to win. To do this you'll need to blend in with everyone else, sneak around using vents, and pin the blame on others.

Nintendo Switch Controls

You can use the touchscreen to play the game or the left Thumbstick to move around. Press "A" to use items, "Y" to report, and "ZL" to bring up the Map. Note that Switch players will also need a paid-for Nintendo Switch Online membership to play online games with others.

LOCAL AND ONLINE GAMES

There are three different ways to play Among Us: Freeplay, Local and Online modes. Each option allows players to tackle the game in a variety of ways for the best murder mystery experience!

Freeplay

This is a great starter option for noobs as you can select from any of the game's three maps and tackle them in single player mode. This mode allows you to safely explore the levels without worrying about being killed. You have as much time as you need to find locations and vents, as well as complete all objectives and sabotage. There are also a number of dummy Crewmates dotted around each map, so you can practise being a sneaky Impostor too!

Local

This option allows players to set up their own games for anyone else who's on the same Wi-Fi network as they are. The player that sets up the game is the Host and their name appears under 'Available Games' in the Local menu option screen. As with Online sessions of Among Us, up to 10 players can take part in the same Local game, but you can play with just two people. You might find it a little easy though ...

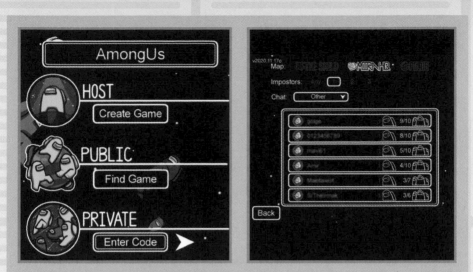

Online

You can host your own games in Among Us or join others from the Online menu screen. If you're setting up a game you can go 'Private' and invite friends with a six digit code, or 'Public' and team up with players from all over the planet. As well as tweaking the game's settings, you can kick rude players out of a session or ban them from your room.

Hosting

As the Host, there are a number of options that allow you to customise your session. You can choose which map to play on, the maximum number of Impostors in the game (up to three), the chat language and the maximum number of players (up to 10).

Codes

In both Public and Private Online matches, a special six digit code is randomly generated at the start of a game. This can be shared with other players to allow them to join in with that session. If a player is kicked out or banned from the room, they won't be able to join again, even with the code. Play nicely and be friendly!

CHARACTER AND GAME SETTINGS

Although setting up a Local or Online game is easy enough, there are lots of settings that players can change to customise sessions. These can affect how a game is played and set certain limits on characters.

Character

Bored of how your character looks? As soon as a new session starts, just hop on over to the laptop in the spawn area and either tap on it or press the 'Customize' button at the bottom right of the screen. Here you'll be able to change the colour and skin of your character, give them a pet and even swap hats!

Custom Settings
Map: MIRA HQ
Impostors: 1 (Limit: 0)
Confirm Ejects: On
Emergency Meetings: 1
Anonymous Votes: Off
Emergency Cooldown: 0s
Discussion Time: 15s
Voting Time: 120s
Player Speed: 1x
Crewmate Vision: 1x
Impostor Vision: 1.5x
Kill Cooldown: 45s
Kill Distance: Normal
Task Bar Updates: Always
Visual Tasks: On
Common Tasks: 1
Long Tasks: 1
Short Tasks: 2

Ping: 50 ms

AmongUs

START

1/10

Pick A Role

On the menu screen, select the 'Game' tab to bring up a number of options. These settings can alter how a game is played and help to crank up the suspense levels, such as the amount of time to vote and how fast players can move. Once you've decided on the options you want, exit the menu and your game settings appear on the left-hand side of the screen and stay there for all players to see.

Advanced Settings

As well as the ability to switch maps, increase the number of Impostors, change player speed and select anonymous Voting (see page 54), these options are worth exploring in more detail:

Confirm Ejects

When voting is done, one player is ejected into space and becomes a Ghost. The game says who the player was, whether they were an Impostor and how many (if any) Impostors remain. Select 'Confirm Ejects' and the Impostor information is kept secret.

Emergency Meetings

Usually called when players discover something suspicious, such as a dead body or someone acting strangely. Players only have a set number of times that they can press the button, but this can be increased to a maximum of nine.

Discussion Time

Once an Emergency Meeting has been called, all living players chat with each other to share clues or try to pin the blame on others. A shorter Discussion Time requires everyone to think very quickly, while the maximum time limit can be set to 120 seconds.

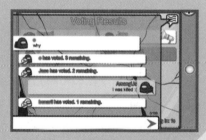

Crewmate/Impostor Vision

It's important to be able see what's near you, as you never know what's lurking round a corner! A player's field of vision can be changed in the settings up to five times for maximum range, handy for spotting sneaky Impostors.

How to Play: Crewmate

When starting a new game, players are randomly assigned one of two roles. If you're a Crewmate, it's your job to stay alive as long as possible, complete tasks and unmask those evil alien Impostors!

Complete Tasks

Crewmates are each given a set of special objectives to complete on every level. Once each task is done, the Total Tasks Completed gauge at the top left of the screen fills up green and the Crewmates win the game. Failure to complete tasks will let the Impostors win. Moreover, Ghosts can continue to complete tasks, allowing Crewmembers to win even if the Impostors are killing everyone.

React to Sabotage

Impostors will attempt to sabotage various sections of each level. Crewmates can choose to ignore the sabotage or fix it. If a Crewmate spots someone doing any sabotage, they should let other players know what they've seen during a Discussion. When an act of sabotage has been committed, players are unable to press the Emergency Meeting button, unless doors have been sabotaged.

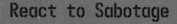

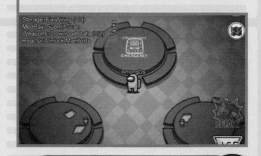

Among Us Fact:

When a Crewmate is killed by an Impostor, all that's left of them is half a body with a bone sticking out. Urgh!

Report Dead Bodies

If Crewmates witness a kill, or if they find a dead body, they should immediately report it to the rest of the Crew. On touchscreen devices, the 'Report' button is located in the bottom right of the screen, for PC users its the 'R' key and for Switch players it's 'Y'. You have to be close to a body to report it and this will trigger a meeting with all surviving players.

Call Emergency Meetings

When a dead body is reported or the Emergency Meeting button is pressed, the game pauses and all players meet up to discuss what they've seen. During a meeting players can use the text chat function at the top right of the screen to tell each other what's been going on, before moving on to vote on who they think is an Impostor.

Check for Suspicious Activity

During games, Crewmates need to keep an eye on what other players are up to. If they're acting strangely, causing sabotage or killing other players, then they're an Impostor! Crewmates can check security cameras, Doorlogs and the Admin map to see where other players are and what they're doing. If anything looks dodgy, Crewmates should head back to the Cafeteria and hit the Emergency Meeting Button.

Ghosts

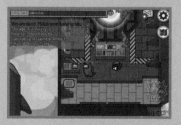

Players that are killed become Ghosts. They are invisible, have the ability to move through walls and can still do tasks to help others win. However, they're unable to start Emergency Meetings, fix sabotage, report dead bodies or chat with living players during Discussions.

How to Play: Impostor

Up to three Impostors can take part in a game and sneak around levels, killing off Crewmates. This involves sabotage, blaming others for your actions and making sure no one discovers you're a parasitic shapeshifter!

Kill Off The Crew

Depending on each game's settings, Impostors have to get within a certain distance of a Crewmate to end their life. Once an Impostor has dispatched a Crewmate, there's a kill cooldown period. Impostors can't then kill more Crewmates until the timer has run down. If there are the same amount of Impostors as Crewmates before all Crew tasks are completed, the Impostors win.

Blend In With The Crew

To avoid being suspected and ejected, Impostors have to be clever and act as if they're actually one of the Crew. Start behaving suspiciously or get caught doing something you shouldn't and you may get found out. Impostors look exactly the same as Crewmates, so it's impossible for other players to tell if they're an alien until they kill, sabotage or do anything to raise the alarm.

Sneak Through Vents

There are multiple vents located in each level and Impostors can use these to hide in or to quickly move around the map. Crewmates can't see you in vents unless they access the Admin Map, and then they'll know exactly where you are!

Pretend To Run Tasks

At the start of a game, Impostors are given a list of fake tasks shown at the top left of their screen. Players can then stand in the area where a task has to be completed and hang around for a few seconds, pretending to Crewmates that they're not an Impostor.

Sabotage The Ship

Impostors can open up a red map showing areas that can be sabotaged. Players can select which sabotage they want to do and the Crew will ignore or attempt to fix it. Once sabotage begins, Crewmates are unable to stop the Emergency Button from being pressed, unless doors have been sabotaged.

Close Doors and Trap Crewmates

On The Skeld and Polus maps, it's possible to trap Crewmates by sabotaging the doors. The doors are marked on the map by a circle round it and a red 'X' in the centre. Crewmates either have to fix the doors on The Skeld or reset four switches on Polus to reactivate them. After an Emergency Meeting in The Skeld, the doors will automatically reopen.

Ghosts

Impostors who are ejected become Ghosts. As with Crewmates, they are invisible, can travel through walls and do tasks. However, they can no longer kill Crewmates. Impostors can chat with other Impostor Ghosts, but not live players. The game must be set to two Impostors for there to be Impostor Ghosts.

SABOTAGE

Impostors can cause all sorts of trouble for players by breaking, deactivating or locking certain areas on each map. It's up to Crewmates to work together to reverse the sabotage before the alien can strike again!

Sabotage Map

Impostors (and Impostor Ghosts) can bring up a red sabotage map that shows which areas can be affected. By tapping on an icon in an area, players will activate an alarm and the screen flashes red to show that something is wrong. Impostors can only do one type of sabotage at a time, except for Door Sabotage, which can be activated while other sabotage is occurring.

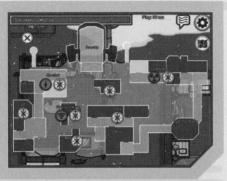

O₂ Oxygen Depletion

This is a major problem and Crewmates need to act quickly to stop the countdown reaching zero. To shut down the sabotage, head over to either O2 or Admin on The Skeld map, or the Greenhouse on MIRA HQ, then tap in the correct codes on the PIN pads.

☢ Reactor Meltdown

If you let the Reactor fully melt down, your ship or HQ will be destroyed! Two Crewmates need to work together and head to the Reactor where they'll find two fingerprint scanners. Both players must hold their hands on the scanners at the same time.

☢ Reset Seismic Stabilizers

Polus has its own unique sabotage event – Reset Seismic Stabilizers. This is similar to Reactor Meltdown, but players have more time to activate the two fingerprint scanners and stop the base from being destroyed.

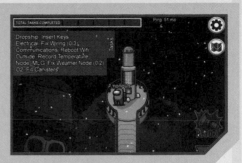

📶 Comms Sabotage

This sabotage stops Crewmates from viewing their task lists and deactivates Security, Vitals, Admin map and Doorlog. To fix on The Skeld and Polus, just turn the comms dial to match the other signal. On MIRA HQ, two players have to enter PIN codes in the Office and Communications.

⚡ Fix Lights

When triggered, players' vision is reduced, giving Impostors an opportunity for a kill. To fix the lights, flip the circuit breaker switches in Electrical (or the Office in MIRA HQ) until the lights above each switch turn green.

✳ Door Sabotage

Impostors can lock Crewmates in or out of rooms for 10 seconds with this sabotage. They'll automatically reopen after that time, except on Polus. Here you'll need to reset four switches on a circuit breaker to get them working again.

Among Us Fact: Did you know that Reset Seismic Stabilizers is the only sabotage in the game that gives you 60 seconds to fix?

CREWMATE TASKS

There are a number of objectives for Crewmates (and Ghosts) to complete to win the game. Every time a task is completed, the Total Tasks Completed bar at the top left of the screen will fill up.

Accept Diverted Power and Divert Power

Location: Electrical, Reactor   Various

This is a two-part task that's super-easy to do! Flip a switch all the way up in Electrical or Reactor, then go to the highlighted room to accept the power.

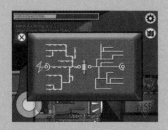

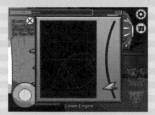

Align Engine Output

Location: Lower Engine, Upper Engine

With the engines out of alignment, the ship isn't going anywhere. Complete this two-part task by moving the slider arrow up and down to successfully line up the engine with the horizontal red dotted line.

Align Telescope

Location: Laboratory

It's time to go object spotting in space! Take a look through the telescope and move it around to find the highlighted item at the bottom right of the screen. A beeping sound increases the closer you are to the correct object.

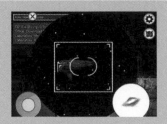

Assemble Artifact

Location: Laboratory

Select the various purple gem pieces and then place them in the correct order in the centre of the screen to successfully complete the strange crystal.

Buy Beverage

Location: Cafeteria

All of those objectives and sabotage can be thirsty work! Choose the correct drink from the vending machine by pressing the letter and number combination keys. Tap the green tick button when done to enjoy your tasty beverage.

Calibrate Distributor

Location: Electrical

This task will take timing and quick reflexes. On the left-hand side of the screen are three coloured nodes rotating anti-clockwise. When the grey part of the node reaches the empty bar on the right-hand side, press the correct button below it.

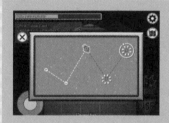

Chart Course

Location: Navigation   Admin   Dropship

Get ready for blast off by working out where you're going! Press the panel to bring up a computer display screen, then move the spaceship icon from point to point until you reach your final destination.

Clean O2 Filter

Location: O2   Greenhouse

This is a very simple task that can be completed quickly. Just drag six brown leaves to the trash slot. The leaves only require a slight push towards the trash for them to float in.

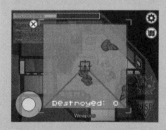

Clear Asteroids

Location: Weapons   Balcony

Destroy 20 asteroids by tapping or clicking on them as they float past on the green screen. Asteroids will be blasted with lasers and then disappear.

CREWMATE TASKS

Download/Upload Data

Location: 🔴 🟡 🟢 Various

Head on over to the location on the Map and press the Download button, then go to the second location to Upload the data and complete the task.

Enter ID Code

Location: 🟡 Admin

Pull out the white ID card in the Crewmate's wallet, then tap in the code on it by using the keypad. When you've finished entering the code, press the green tick button.

Empty Garbage/Chute

Location: 🔴 🟡 Cafeteria 🟢 O2

Pull and hold the lever on the right-hand side to empty the leaves in the chute. This is a two-part task in The Skeld and Polus.

Fill Cannisters

Location: 🟢 O2

Start by moving the empty cannister at the top of the screen and aligning it with the airway below. There are two cannisters to be filled in total.

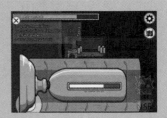

Fix Weather Node

Location: 🟢 Laboratory, Outside

Head over to one of the six nodes shown on the Map and then guide a cursor through a maze. Finally go to the Laboratory to switch the node on.

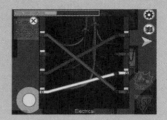
Fix Wiring

Location: Various

Head to the locations shown on the Map and tap the electricial panel. Connect matching coloured wires by dragging them from one side of the screen to the other.

Fuel Engines

Location: Various   Lower Engine

Fill the cannister up with fuel by pressing and holding the button down. Then take the cannister to the Engines to fuel them and complete the task.

Insert Keys

Location: Dropship

Select the key on the keyring and move it to the correct slot on the right. Once inserted, turn the key 90 degrees. Check out the funny alien pet keyring decoration!

Inspect Sample

Location: MedBay

Start by pressing the green button at the bottom of the screen, wait for 59 seconds then press the button below the red sample.

Measure Weather

Location: Balcony

This is one of the simplest tasks to complete. Press the Begin button on the screen and wait until the message 'Done' appears. You'll have successfully measured the weather and finished another task.

CREWMATE TASKS

Monitor Tree

Location: 02

Move the four coloured sliders up and down to match the CO2, NUTRI, RAD and WATER thresholds shown on the screen. When all four sliders have reached the correct place, the task has been completed.

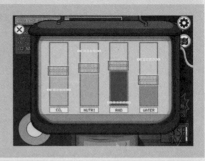

Open Waterways

Location: Boiler Room, Outside

First head on over to the Boiler Room and open the valves by spinning the large wheels. Once that's done go back outside near the Office to open up the last valve.

Prime Shields

Location: Shields   Admin

This is a very simple visual task that can be completed very quickly. Just click or tap on the red hexagons on the screen. Once they're all white, the task will be finished.

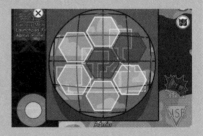

Process Data

Location: Office

To Process Data, head to the Office in MIRA HQ and tap on the computer screen. Next press the Upload button and wait 12 seconds for the data to begin processing. Watch your back if you're attempting this task as it may leave you open to attack.

Reboot Wifi

Location: Communications

Pull the red lever down to start a 60 second countdown. Once finished, pull the lever back up to complete the task. This is one of the longest tasks in the game.

Record Temperature

Location: Laboratory, Outside

Click or hold the green arrow keys up and down to enter the correct temperature reading shown on the screen. Once the two numbers match, you're all done.

Repair Drill

Location: Laboratory

Click on the four red corners of the computer screen until they all completely disappear. The on-screen text will then display 'Status: FINE' and the task is done.

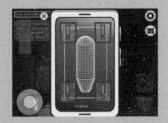

Replace Water Jug

Location: Boiler Room, Office

First of all, head on over to the Boiler Room and fill up a water jug by pressing the button. Now go to the Office and do the same thing again.

Run Diagnostics

Location: Launch pad

Press the space bar on the computer keyboard to find any anomalies on the ship. Wait 90 seconds then press the red location to finish.

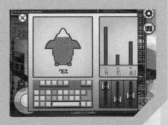

CREWMATE TASKS

Scan Boarding Pass

Location: 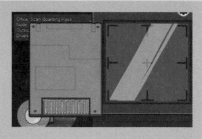 Office

Begin by pressing the yellow triangle to show the boarding pass and then the arrow to flip it over. Now drag the boarding pass on to the scanner until it's green to complete the task.

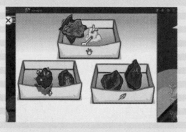

Sort Samples

Location: Laboratory

There are six different sample items to place in three bins, each of which has a logo on the front. Your task is to match all of the items to the correct logos and place them in the bins.

Stabilise Steering

Location: Navigation

Drag the white indicator to the centre of the computer screen so that it lines up with the crosshair. It will blink green when complete and the ship's steering will have been successfully stabilised.

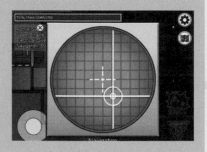

Start Reactor

Location: Reactor   Specimen Room

This task can take a little while, so make sure that you're safe before starting! You have to memorise the flashing pattern of blue squares and then repeat them with the keypad. Keep going until all the lights flash green.

Store Artifacts

Location: Specimen Room

Pick up and place the four strange items into the correct empty holes in the artifact case. Each object has to precisely match the hole shape.

Submit Scan

Location: MedBay

To start this task, stand on the platform to initiate the MedBay scan. Only Crewmates can do this task and it proves to others that they're not an Impostor.

Swipe Card

Location: Admin   Office

Take the white ID card out of the Crewmate's wallet and swipe it through the scanner at the correct speed. If you're too slow or fast you'll have to swipe it again.

Unlock Manifolds

Location: Reactor   Specimen Room

To unlock the ship's manifolds, tap in the numbers 1 to 10 on the keypad in the correct order. If you make a mistake, you'll have to start all over again.

Water Plants

Location: Greenhouse, Storage

First collect a watering can from Storage and then head on over to the Greenhouse, where you'll find four house plants. Tap on each of the four plants to successfully water them.

THE SKELD MAP

The first map to be included with the game, The Skeld is set on a ship in outer space. Its design and tasks have made it very popular with Among Us players.

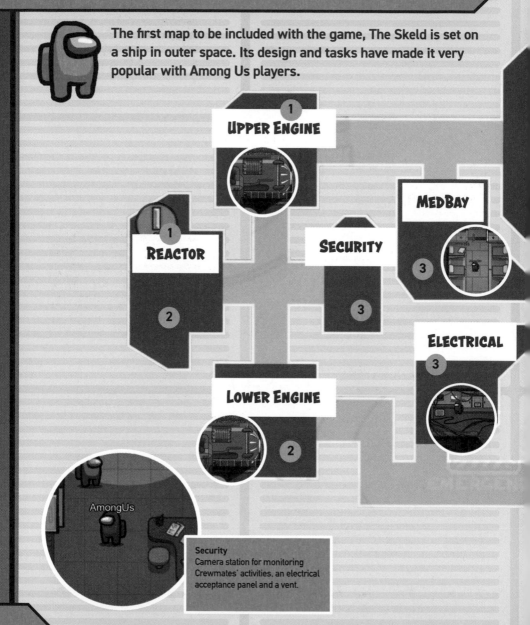

UPPER ENGINE 1

REACTOR 1 2

SECURITY 3

MEDBAY 3

ELECTRICAL 3

LOWER ENGINE 2

AmongUs

Security
Camera station for monitoring Crewmates' activities, an electrical acceptance panel and a vent.

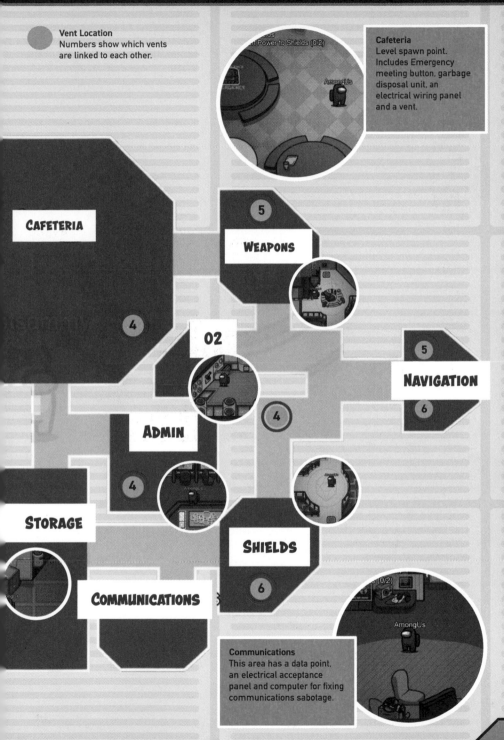

Vent Location
Numbers show which vents are linked to each other.

Cafeteria
Level spawn point. Includes Emergency meeting button, garbage disposal unit, an electrical wiring panel and a vent.

AmongUs

CAFETERIA

5

WEAPONS

02

4

5

NAVIGATION

6

ADMIN

4

4

STORAGE

SHIELDS

COMMUNICATIONS

6

Communications
This area has a data point, an electrical acceptance panel and computer for fixing communications sabotage.

AmongUs

THE SKELD: LEVEL GUIDE CREWMATE

Initially the only map available in the game, The Skeld is the most popular level in Among Us. To survive as a Crewmate you'll need to know all of the secrets this map contains …

Spawn Point

All players begin the game in the Cafeteria near the table that has the Emergency Meeting Button. Once play begins, everyone goes their separate ways to complete tasks as Crewmates or get up to no good as an Impostor. There are three corridors branching out from the Cafeteria leading to MedBay and the Upper Engine, Storage, Admin and Weapons.

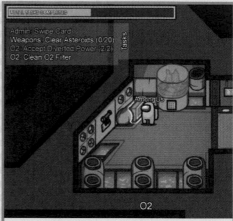

Quickly Tackle Tasks

You'll want to try and get a few tasks under your belt before anyone is killed or any sabotage happens. Head to your first task and complete it as soon as possible. Remember that you're working against the clock to fill your Tasks Completed bar as quickly as you can. The more Crewmates that are dispatched by Impostors, the less time you'll have to do the tasks.

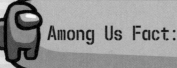

Among Us Fact: When playing the game during Halloween 2019 and 2020, developer Innersloth added spooky extras to The Skeld such as spiders, webs, bats and pumpkins!

MedBay Team-Up

Crewmates should always try and get themselves verified as human in front of another player. Try to follow a fellow Crewmate to MedBay straight away and watch each other be scanned. This way you'll be able to confirm one another's innocence in Discussions and keep an eye out for any sneaky Impostors popping out of the vent for a quick kill.

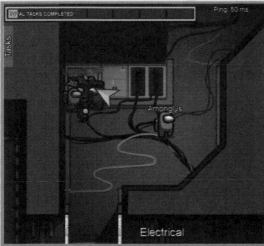

Electrical Death Trap

The Skeld often includes a number of tasks to complete in Electrical, but this is sometimes an ideal place for Impostors to lurk so they can carry out multiple kills at once. It's best to only go there if there are at least two other Crewmates present. While there's a danger that both may actually be Impostors, the chances are they'll back you up while you do your tasks.

Fix Lights

Impostors often cause trouble for Crewmates by sabotaging the lights. This usually means they're going for a quick kill, as the Crewmates' vision is greatly reduced. To prevent this, travel in pairs to fix the multiple light panels located around the level. One of you can repair them, while the other stands guard against lurking Impostors.

THE SKELD: LEVEL GUIDE IMPOSTOR

When tackling The Skeld as an Impostor, there are number of handy ways to successfully kill Crewmates and avoid detection. With practice you'll soon become a master of stealth takedowns!

Essential Sabotage

Although Impostors have a number of sabotage options available to them, choose the Reactor and Oxygen options first. Crewmates can't simply ignore these events as time will be against them. You'll know most Crewmates will be heading to fix the sabotage, giving you a number of kill options and locations.

Communications

Admin

Take Out Comms

Some Crewmates like to wait out the game by staying in Security and watching the monitors until they see someone up to no good. If you take out Communications early on in the game, this will disable the cameras and force Crewmates out of Security, giving you a chance to take them out undetected by other players.

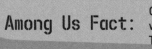

Among Us Fact: On April Fool's Day 2020, Innersloth reversed the whole map so that the ship was flying backwards. The name of the level also changed to 'ehT dlekS'!

Vent System

To avoid being detected by Crewmates, Impostors can use the 14 floor vents in The Skeld to hide and quickly travel from location to location after a kill. Try to get rid of Crewmates and then pop into a vent without being spotted entering or exiting. If you do get caught, simply pin the blame on other players in the Discussion!

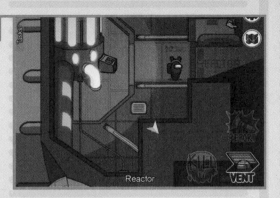

Reactor

Electrical

Lights Out

Sabotage the lights early on for a quick kill. While Crewmates are scrabbling around in the dark with limited vision, you can sneak in and easily take them out. The vision for both Crewmates and Impostors is set by the Host at the start of a game, but the less a Crewmate has the better it is for you get rid of them.

Download Distraction

Follow a Crewmate to Electrical and wait for them to do the Download Data task. As the task window is quite big, you'll have a chance to vent to Security or MedBay for a fast kill, then take the vent back to Electrical before they notice you're gone. You'll have a handy alibi to use when someone reports the body.

Electrical — My Tablet

42%

Estimated Time: 29m 51s

Electrical

MIRA HQ MAP

The second map to be released for Among Us, MIRA HQ is set high up in the Earth's atmosphere and owned by the mysterious MIRA company.

REACTOR

Storage
Small room full of various material near the Cafeteria. Location of watering can for the water the plants task.

DECONTAMINATION

on

1

LAUNCH PAD

1

Launch Pad
The starting spawn point for the level. This area includes the dropship, a diagnostic computer, a refuel station and a vent.

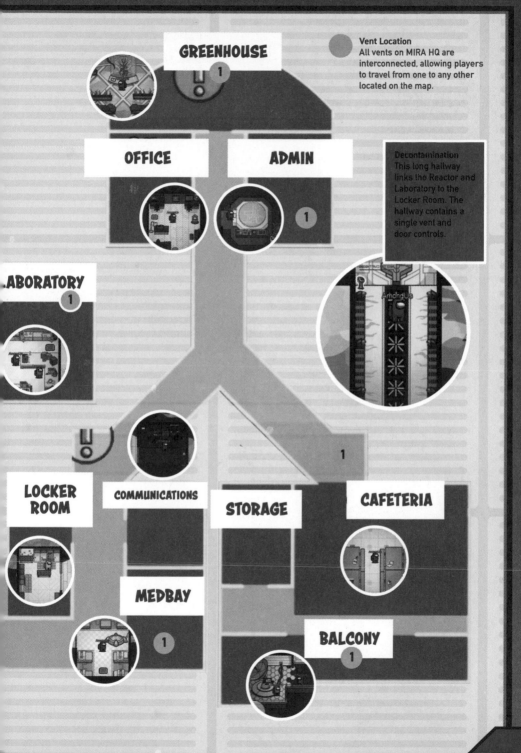

GREENHOUSE

1

Vent Location
All vents on MIRA HQ are interconnected, allowing players to travel from one to any other located on the map.

OFFICE

ADMIN

1

Decontamination
This long hallway links the Reactor and Laboratory to the Locker Room. The hallway contains a single vent and door controls.

LABORATORY

1

LOCKER ROOM

COMMUNICATIONS

STORAGE

1

CAFETERIA

MEDBAY

1

BALCONY

1

MIRA HQ: LEVEL GUIDE CREWMATE

MIRA HQ is a compact level that can take players a short time to cross from one side of the map to the other. Crewmates will need to be extra careful when exploring this floating base!

Check Doorlogs

MIRA HQ is the only map in the game that doesn't have security cameras, but there is a Doorlog system. Head to Communications to check the Doorlogs and see if the movement of any players looks suspicious, as they may be an Impostor. Be aware that Impostors can sabotage Communications, which wipes out the Doorlogs and their recent movements.

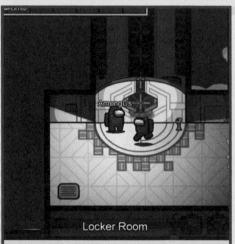

Locker Room

Communications

Unlocked Doors

It isn't possible for Impostors to sabotage any of the doors in MIRA HQ, which Crewmates can use to their advantage. This allows you free access to all of the rooms in the level and you'll be able to easily run away from any Impostors. The only place where doors become an issue is in the Decontamination corridor where you have to wait for both sets to open.

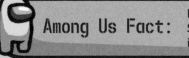

Among Us Fact: MIRA HQ is the only level not to have Door Sabotage, is the smallest map in the game and it has the least number of visual tasks.

Tricky Visual Task

There's only one way for Crewmates to get verified in MIRA HQ and that's to go to MedBay and Submit Scan. This can take a while though, leaving you open for surprise Impostor attacks. Try this visual task in groups of two or more, so one of you can be scanned while others keep an eye out for Impostors nearby.

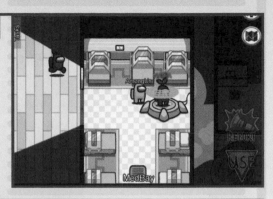

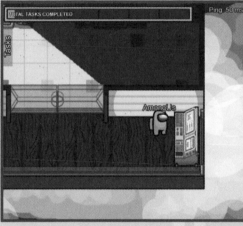

Locations To Avoid

There are two places in MIRA HQ that Crewmates will want to avoid. Try to get into and out of the Launch pad as quickly as you can. If you die here, it can be a while before your body is discovered. The other is the Balcony as it's a remote spot that players only visit to do the Measure Weather task and is the perfect place for an Impostor to hide a quick kill.

Monitor Reactor

If an Impostor sabotages the Reactor in this level, it's essential you get to it quickly and repair the damage. The Reactor room can be tricky to reach if you're in the Greenhouse or Cafeteria and you'll be racing against the clock to get there in time. The Decontamination corridor also slows down access to the Reactor, so try to get through it as fast as you can.

MIRA HQ: LEVEL GUIDE IMPOSTOR

If there's one map in Among Us that gives Impostors a real advantage, it's MIRA HQ. Players can quickly take vents from room to room and take out Crewmates in a number of remote locations.

Launch pad Kills

The spawn point for this level is the launch pad. Once a game starts, Crewmates will dash off in to MIRA HQ to tackle tasks. If you wait around the launch pad, they'll eventually return to complete some of those tasks, giving you the opportunity to kill them and then quickly vent away. As the launch pad is remote, chances are you'll get away with it.

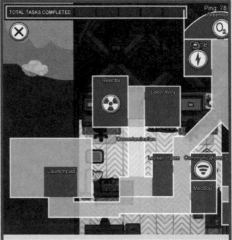

Keep Sabotaging

As some locations in MIRA HQ are quite spread out, it's important to keep sabotaging. This ensures Crewmates have to constantly move around the level to fix your tampering and allows Impostors more opportunities for kills. Crewmates will be so busy sorting out your sabotage and doing their own tasks that they can easily forget to watch out who's near them ...

Among Us Fact: Look closely in the Office and you'll see a poster on the wall for 'The Henry Stickmin Collection', a series of games also developed by Innersloth!

Fast Vent Travel

Due to the layout of MIRA HQ, using the vent system on this level allows Impostors to travel very quickly from room to room. The vents form one large loop around the level, allowing speedy movement to avoid detection. However, note that there are no vents in the Locker Room, Communications, Storage or the Cafeteria.

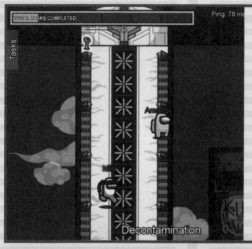

Decontamination Kill Avoidance

Impostors may be tempted to kill Crewmates in the Decontamination corridor, but this is best avoided. When both sets of doors are closed, there's an opportunity to get rid of a Crewmate trapped with you before escaping via the vents. But with an entrance on either side of the corridor, there's a good chance that you'll be spotted by players waiting at the doors and be caught in the act.

Don't Hide For Too Long

Although the vent system in MIRA HQ is handy for Impostors, it can also catch you out. Spend too long hiding in vents and other players may become suspicious. Make sure to hop out of the vents now and again to fake tasks or show other players that you're still active.

POLUS MAP

Set on an alien world, this planetary base is the third map in the game and is known as both Polus Outpost and Planet Polus.

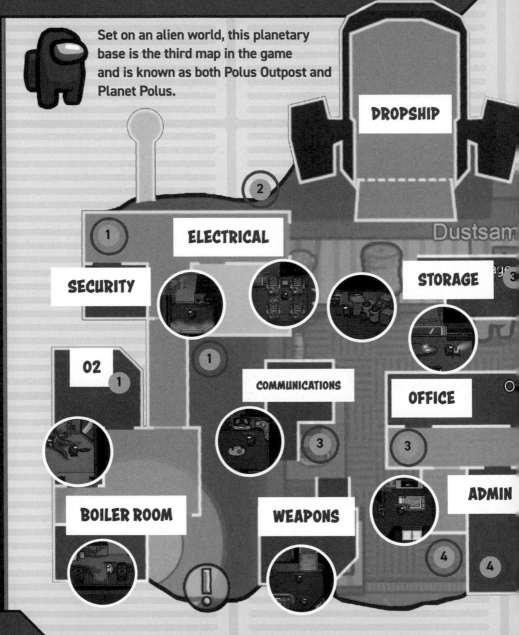

DROPSHIP

2

1

ELECTRICAL

SECURITY

STORAGE

3

O2

1

1

COMMUNICATIONS

OFFICE

3

3

ADMIN

BOILER ROOM

WEAPONS

4

4

Dustsam

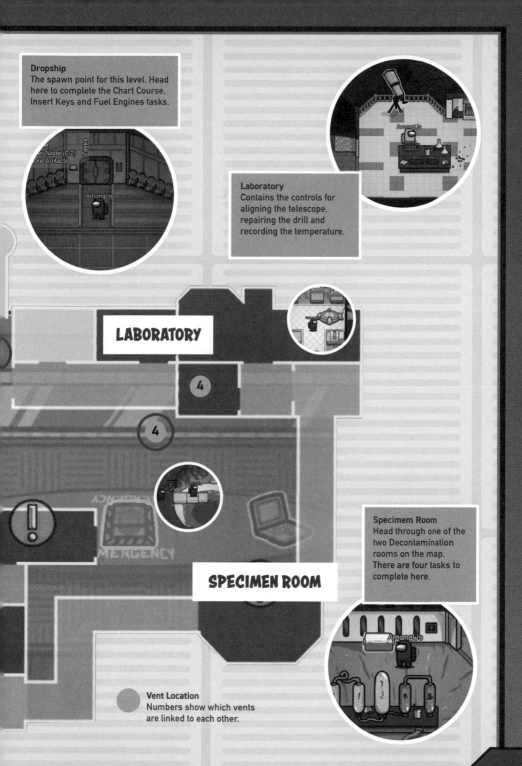

Dropship
The spawn point for this level. Head here to complete the Chart Course, Insert Keys and Fuel Engines tasks.

Laboratory
Contains the controls for aligning the telescope, repairing the drill and recording the temperature.

LABORATORY

SPECIMEN ROOM

Specimem Room
Head through one of the two Decontamination rooms on the map. There are four tasks to complete here.

Vent Location
Numbers show which vents are linked to each other.

POLUS: LEVEL GUIDE CREWMATE

The alien world of Polus provides many challenges for Crewmates, both inside the base and outside on the strange surface of the planet. Just be sure to watch your back at all times!

Use Cameras

As soon as the game starts, head over to the left-hand side of the map to Security. Here you'll be able to access one of six cameras located around the level. These are handy for finding dead bodies or players acting suspiciously. However, unlike on The Skeld, you can only view one camera at a time, leaving you open to sneak attacks.

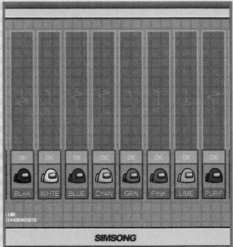

SIMSONG

East

Keep An Eye on Vitals

One handy ability Crewmates have on this map is they're able to check on the health of fellow players. Go to the Office and use Vitals to check out which Crewmates are still alive. If someone is dead, but no body has been reported, sound the alarm or look nearby to try and find potential Impostors who may be trying to escape the scene.

Among Us Fact: When players are ejected on Polus, they're dropped in to lava. Crewmates reach out a hand before sinking and Impostors give a final thumbs up!

Stay Inside

If your Crewmate tasks allow it, try to stay indoors as much as possible. There's a lot of open terrain and remote areas out on the planet's surface where a dead body might not be discovered for a while. This allows any Impostors to kill off even more Crewmates before someone manages to rise the alarm.

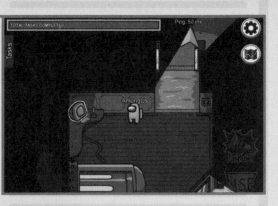

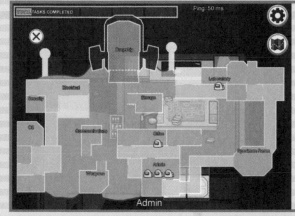

Check Admin Map

As well as the monitors in Security and Vitals in the Office, there's another useful Crewmate tool in this level. Make your way to Admin and access the computer map of Polus. This will show you where Crewmates are located and you can also see if any Impostors pop up from vents or if players disappear when killed.

It's A Trap!

There are a couple of locations on the map where you can get separated from Crewmates and be ambushed by an Impostor. These include O2, the Specimen Room and the Seismic Stabilizers. If possible, only travel to these places with others when trying to complete tasks as you may need strength in numbers.

POLUS: LEVEL GUIDE IMPOSTOR

Sneaky parasitic alien shapeshifters should feel right at home on this weird alien planet! Follow the tips below to successfully take out plenty of unsuspecting Crewmates.

Door Traps

The doors on Polus don't automatically open after a short while as they do on The Skeld. Instead Crewmates have to manually open them, giving you plenty of time to kill. One handy way to do this is to shut the doors with a Crewmate trapped inside, get rid of them and then vent to safety before other players have time to find the body.

Specimen Room

Specimen Room Kills

This is one location on the map that is quite remote and players can only access it by going through one of two Decontamination corridors. You can't vent to the room, so just follow a Crewmate to the location and then kill them. By the time anyone discovers the dead body, you'll be long gone ...

Among Us Fact: Polus is the only map in Among Us that doesn't have a Cafeteria. However, it does have a toilet in the Laboratory, but unfortunately it's out of order ...

Seismic Stabilizer Lurking

There are two of these on the map, in separate locations. Sabotage them and Crewmates will have to fix the damage before the time runs out. This usually means at least one player has to go to each, making them handy locations for kills. Only try this if the Crewmate is on their own and doesn't report you first.

Crewmate Team-Up

The Polus map is quite large and it can take time to get around it. One sneaky trick to try is to hang around with a Crewmate as they do tasks and build up their loyalty. If there's more than one Impostor in the level, your Crewmate buddy is more likely to defend you in a Discussion if a body is reported. Once they're on your side, move in for the kill!

Always Watching?

You can get caught out on Polus if you're being watched. Look for the six Security cameras around the base and if they have a blinking red light on them. If the light is off, you'll be safe and could go for a kill. The Admin map and Vitals also work against you, so be sure to pick your moments when taking out any Crewmates.

ADVANCED TIPS & TRICKS: CREWMATE

Once you're familiar with the maps and had plenty of practice surviving the game, there are all sorts of advanced strategies for winning as a Crewmate. Try these tactics to improve your odds at staying alive!

Complete Tasks Quickly

Try to finish your tasks as fast as you can. If there are only a few of you left, stay together and complete the tasks as a unit. That way you'll have safety in numbers and might be able to work out who's an Impostor too.

Watch Task Completed Bar

If you're in the same room as someone doing a single part task, the green bar will increase once they've completed it. If it doesn't change, they're faking the task!

Verify Crewmates

If you're near a player who is about to Submit Scan, Prime Shields, Empty Garbage or Clear Asteroids tasks, wait to see if they actually do it. If an animation shows them doing the task, then that player is a Crewmate. If not, then they're an Impostor and faking it.

Verify Yourself

Head to the MedBay and perform a scan, empty the trash chute in Storage, blast asteroids or prime the Shields in front of other players and they'll know you're human.

Stay With Verified Crewmates

Once you know another player is a Crewmate, you can then follow them around safe in the knowledge that they're not going to try and kill you! Of course, they may also think you're an Impostor if you do that, so try and get verified in front of them too.

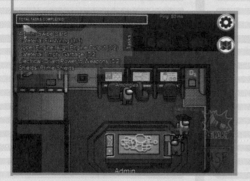

Don't Just Run Around

Make sure you're either doing your tasks as quickly as possible, staying with larger groups of players or not acting suspiciously. Players that are just running around are probably up to no good and waiting for the chance to kill someone.

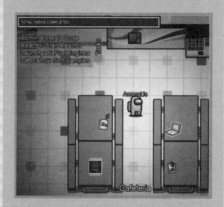

Don't Press The Button

Try to avoid using the Emergency Meeting button unless absolutely necessary. If you press it too early or too often and use up all of your turns, other players may become suspicious and decide to vote you out.

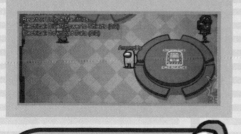

Among Us Tip:

If you're with other Crewmates, watch for players who go off and do their own thing as they may be an Impostor!

Use Security

Head to Security to check live camera feeds and see where players are on the map, except for Impostors hiding in vents. Don't look at the screens for too long though, as you can leave yourself open to a sneak attack while you're busy.

Remember Pairs

Try to keep an eye out for Crewmates travelling in pairs. If one of those Crewmates is killed, then it's a sure bet that the other player with them is an Impostor. If they both use a vent to hide, they're aliens working together.

Use Admin

Admin is also a valuable Crewmate tool. From here you can see the location of living and dead players and watch if anyone quickly moves from place to place using vents. If a player vanishes and then reappears, they've just used a vent.

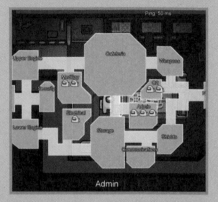

Among Us Tip

If you leave the game for a short period of time, other players may suspect you're faking tasks!

Vitals Strategy

If four players are left on Polus and one Crewmate can confirm the other is human, they should stick together. If they check Vitals and one of the other players dies, then the remaining player will be the Impostor.

Use Doorlog

You can only use this tactic in MIRA HQ, but it can be handy way of discovering Impostors. Head to Communications and access the Doorlog to see who has entered and exited. The logs are wiped if comms are sabotaged.

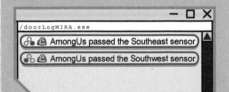

Head Away From Sabotage

If there are enough of you, try heading in the opposite direction when sabotage occurs. An Impostor may have set off the sabotage to draw players away from a dead body. Leave the repairs to your Crewmates and you can look for anything suspicious.

Always Report Dead Bodies

If you see a dead body, always report it as quickly as you can. Chances are the killer is still close by and could be identified in discussion with other players in a meeting. If someone is running away from a body, they're probably an Impostor!

Defend Other Crewmates

When you're in a meeting and someone is being accused, use any evidence you have to either defend them or back up the accusation. Many innocent Crewmates are often ejected by mistake, so make sure you have your teammate's backs.

Have An Alibi

If you're the person being accused, make sure you have your story straight. If you've not acted suspiciously in front of others and shown you can be trusted, then you don't need to worry about being voted out.

Accusers Who Die

Try to remember in meetings who has accused who. If an accuser turns up dead later on, then they may have been killed by the player they pointed the finger at. This tactic is a lot easier to try when there are fewer players left in the game.

ADVANCED TIPS & TRICKS: IMPOSTOR

Being a parasitic alien Impostor involves being super-sneaky and deceptive. If you can trick, trap and fool other players without being caught, then you'll be victorious in every single game. Here's how to do it!

Travelling By Vent

Use the vents to kill and sneak away. Be careful not to hop in or out of vents when Crewmates are nearby and don't stay in them too long, just in case you're spotted moving quickly by someone in Admin.

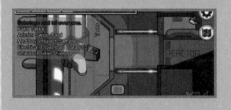

Kill Distances

You may have to get close up to a Crewmate to kill them, depending on the distance that has been set for each game by the Host. The closer you are to a Crewmate, the more chance they'll suspect you're an Impostor.

Watch Out For Cameras

Look for cameras on the walls of some rooms in The Skeld and Polus maps. If a light on them is blinking red, you're being watched by someone in Security, so be careful.

Know When To Kill

You'll need practise to take out other players effectively. Take your time, wait until a Crewmate is on their own, then move in for the kill. If you don't feel like the time is right, leave the room and find another victim somewhere else.

Sabotage During Kill Cooldowns

After a kill, there is a cooldown period before you can get rid of any more Crewmates. Use this time to sabotage the level and then move in for another kill while players are distracted and fixing the problem you've caused.

Keep Sabotaging

The sabotage map allows you to cause mayhem from anywhere. Keep an eye on the cooldown time for the game you're in before you sabotage again. The more you keep the Crewmates on their toes, the more chances you'll have for kills.

Players Remaining

The longer the game lasts, the less players there will be. Try to keep track of how many other players remain by using the Security and Admin rooms. Once there are the same number of Impostors as Crewmates, you'll have won the game.

Quickly Kill Verified Players

If you're with one other Crewmate and they perform a task to get verified (Submit Scan, Prime Shields, Empty Garbage or Clear Asteroids), they'll expect you to then do the same. The best tactic here is just to kill them straight away.

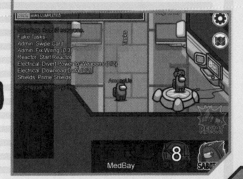

Among Us Tip:

If a Crewmate is on their own and goes to hit the Emergency Meeting Button, take them out quickly and then vent away!

Head to Sabotage

When you perform sabotage, head over to that area to avoid arousing suspicion. Any players that join you will usually think you're a Crewmate trying to fix the problem. If there's just two of you there, go in for the quick kill.

Don't Fake For Too Long

Pretend to do Crewmate tasks to fool other players into thinking you're on their side. Take too long doing a fake task or if a Crewmate realises the task isn't actually being done then you'll be in big trouble.

Among Us Tip:

Sabotage the lights in a level, perform a quick kill in the dark, then vent to fix the lights. No one will suspect it was you!

Blame Others

In Discussions, point the finger of blame at innocent players and try to convince everyone to vote them out. This doesn't always work if they have a good alibi, but it can get others ejected for your deeds!

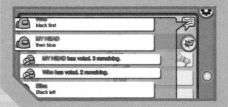

Self-Reporting

Throw Crewmates off your scent by reporting kills that you do yourself. Be careful though as someone may be watching in Security or Admin. If you do this too many times in one match, other players will be very suspicious.

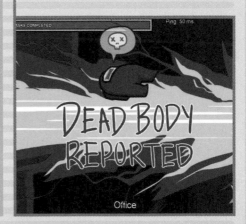

Stack Kill

This is a slightly risky strategy, but it can work in your favour. When in larger groups of players all huddled together, see if you can go for a quick kill. In all the confusion others probably won't know who it was and you'll avoid blame.

Have a Confusing Name

If you name your character one colour (such as blue), but your character is actually another colour (red), then this can help confuse players during discussions. Likewise, calling yourself 'Impostor' can be a double bluff that works in your favour!

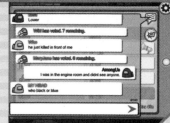

Stick to Your Story

When the time comes for Discussions and Voting, make sure you have a well thought-out alibi. The simplest stories are often the most convincing lies, so stick to the facts and you should manage to avoid getting ejected from the level.

Vote With The Crowd

When it comes to Discussions, keep track of who Crewmates are pointing the finger at. If you're lucky and they don't suspect you, then join in and vote for the player everyone else is going for. This should help draw suspicion away from you.

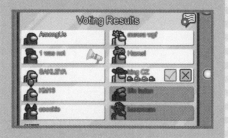

Betray Your Impostor Teammate

During Discussions you don't have to help other Impostors survive. Try pinning the blame on them instead and convince others to vote them out. You won't make many friends that way, but at least you might live long enough to win the game!

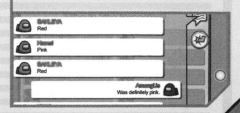

DISCUSSION

 When an Emergency Meeting is triggered, all players gather to discuss what has happened and what they've seen. Everyone then has the option to vote another player out and possibly eject an Impostor.

Meeting Up

There are two parts to this section of the game: Discussion and Voting (see page 56). When the Emergency Meeting button is called, players are transported to the Cafeteria or Office and then go straight into a Discussion. This is a chat room lobby, with an icon showing each player's character and name. Living players are shown on a white background, while any dead players have a large red X through their character icon. You can talk using a mic, or by typing.

Discussion

Clicking on the chat icon on the top right-hand side of the screen brings up a window where players can type text to say whatever they want to each other. Everyone gets to discuss what they may have seen, where they were when the Emergency Meeting was called and who they think the Impostor could be. This is also an opportunity for Impostors to deceive other players and cast suspicion on Crewmates (see page 56).

Time To Chat

Before a game begins, the Host can set the amount of time that players have in a Discussion. If there's very little time to chat in the lobby, players will have to act quickly to make up their minds. More time (up to 120 seconds) gives everyone the chance to work together by adding up all the evidence and figuring out who's been doing what. Players are unable to vote during the Discussion session.

Kicking Players

If someone is being rude to others in a Discussion, it's possible to kick them out of the lobby using the boot icon at the top right of the screen. The Host of a game can do this and also ban players altogether. It's possible for three players to team up to vote and kick a player out of the game, so everyone needs to be on their best behaviour. Note that it's not possible for Ghosts to vote to kick other players out.

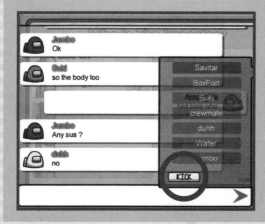

What To Discuss

During the Discussion you can chat about anything from where a dead body was discovered and if anyone was acting suspiciously to where you were on the map and who you suspect the Impostor might be. Players accused of being up to no good can defend themselves and other players can back them up. Try to join in and not stay completely silent though, as that can look suspicious too!

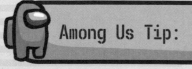

Among Us Tip: Impostors can try to cover for their fellow alien parasites during a Discussion, but Crewmates may remember they did that and then vote them out next time!

VOTING

After the Discussion period is over, players move on to the Voting stage. Every living player gets the chance to choose who they think the Impostor is and the player with the most votes will be ejected from the game!

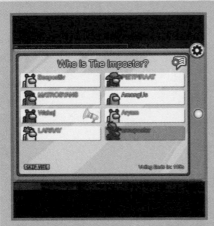

Time to Vote

Voting takes place on the same screen that shows all of the players in the Discussion. After the Discussion time has ended, a voting countdown timer appears and players need to decide who they are going to eject, based on all the evidence they have. As with Discussions, the voting time can be set by the host of the game from between 15-120 seconds. Less time makes the process even more nail-biting!

I Voted!

To cast votes, players have to select the Crewmate they think might actually be an alien Impostor. Two boxes will then appear under that character – a green tick to confirm your selection and a red X to cancel it. Once you have made your vote, you can't then change your selection and choose to vote for a different player. With your vote cast, a little 'I Voted' badge will appear next to your character.

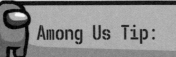

Among Us Tip:
The game ends if only three players remain and one is voted out, regardless of whether they're a Crewmate or Impostor.

Skip Vote

Sometimes during a Discussion, or if players have called an Emergency Meeting too early in the game, it might not always be possible to work out who the Impostor is. When it comes to voting, uncertain players can simply choose to press the grey 'Skip Vote' button on the main Discussion screen and not pick a possible suspect at all. Skip too many times and players may start to suspect you're up to no good ...

Anonymous Voting

If the host has set Anonymous Voting off, then you can see how every other player has voted in the game. If someone says in the Discussion that they're going to vote when one way, but they select a different player, they might just be an Impostor. With Anonymous Voting on it's impossible to see which players anyone has selected, giving Impostors more of an advantage and leaving Crewmates unsure of who's an alien shapeshifter.

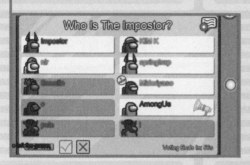

Ejection and Ties

Once all votes have been cast, it's time to reveal the result of everyone's decisions. You'll get to see a player ejected in to space on The Skeld, plummeting through the sky on MIRA HQ or splashing into lava on Polus, along with a message saying if they were a Crewmate or Impostor. In the event of a tie, no one is ejected at all and the game resumes once again.

THE ART OF DECEPTION

If you're playing the game as an Impostor, you're going to need to learn how to successfully deceive other players into thinking you're an innocent Crewmate. There are a number of sneaky ways you can learn to dodge the truth!

Act Like A Detective

When a Discussion begins, immediately take charge of the situation to put Crewmates on the wrong footing. Start asking questions about where everyone else was and what they were up to. You can then begin pressing other players about their actions and begin to suggest to everyone that the player is acting suspiciously and all of the facts point to them being the Impostor instead.

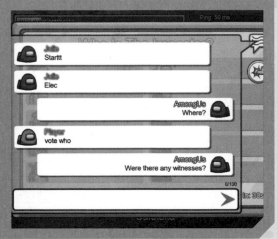

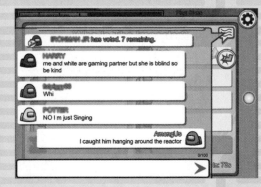

Blame Others

One way of getting out of trouble is to point the finger at other players. For instance, if you kill a Crewmate and another player walks in and catches you, report the dead body yourself and then say the other player did it. Your fellow Crewmates are likely to believe you as you raised the alarm. With any luck they'll then vote to eject that player and you can get even more kills.

Among Us Fact: If someone's suggesting you're an Impostor and you get away with it, don't then kill that player as you'll look very guilty!

Reverse Blame

If the same situation occurred, but the other player reported the dead body first, there's still a way to avoid being voted out. During the Discussion, try to convince the other players that you witnessed the Crewmate killing someone and that they self-reported it. That way the other Crewmate will have to defend themselves, while also trying to pin the blame on you!

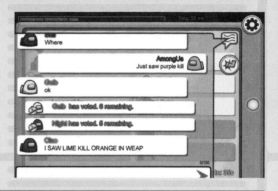

Never Admit Your Guilt

The most important thing to remember is you must never own up to any wrongdoing. Try to craft a story that sounds convincing and makes others doubt what their fellow Crewmates are telling them. If you add a few truthful statements to what you're saying, then your deception will become even more believable. If you take too long to answer questions from Crewmates or make up facts on the spot, you'll be in trouble.

Too Much Deception

On the other hand, too much deception can make other players suspicious. When in a Discussion, don't always blame others for your actions. Crewmates will soon figure out you're trying to deceive them if you're always pointing the finger at other players. Sometimes it's better to keep your comments to a minimum and only speak up when asked a direct question.

SHHHHHHH!

COSMETICS AND PURCHASES

Players can easily customise their Crewmate or Impostor character in the Hub with a variety of different accessories called Cosmetics. Some of these are free, while others cost real money from the in-game store.

In the paid-for PC version of Among Us, nearly all of the Cosmetics are already included with the game, but mobile players must unlock them by spending real money. Cosmetics don't really change the game or a character's abilities, but they're still fun to collect!

Pets

Although not available at launch, Pets were added in a subsequent update that allowed players to have their very own friendly creature. Pets don't actually do anything, but they will follow you around loyally and also remain in the location of your death, if you're killed.

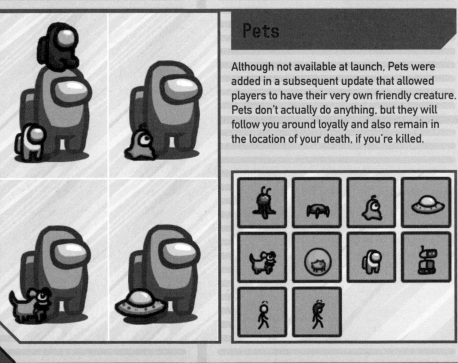

Hats

This selection of cool headgear includes helmets, caps, crowns, halos, masks, and much more. Special items such as the Halloween range of hats are unlocked for a short time once a year and are then unavailable for 12 months.

LIMITED ITEMS

Some Cosmetics are very rare and have only been released by developer Innersloth to mark special occasions. The Party Hat was available for free New Year 2019 and nine secret hats were released on Christmas 2018!

Bundles

If you're looking for a bargain in the store, you could pick up a bundle. These special selections have a number of items combined into one package. They have included the Holiday '18 Hats Bundle, Hats in 1M Bundle and MIRA HQ and Polus Skin Bundle.

Skins

These are costumes that a character wears on their upper and lower body. Some of them look quite practical, while others are just hilarious! From astronaut and mechanic outfits to a doctor and miner, there's a perfect character skin for everyone.

MIRA HQ Skin Bundle

MIRA HQ Skin Bundle

GLOSSARY

Admin
Ability to view the map in the Admin room and see where players are in a level.

Cooldown
An amount of time set by the Host before a player can perform an action again, such as kill.

Cosmetics
Items including hats, pets and skins that players can use to customise the look of their character.

Crewmate
One of two player roles. Crewmates have to perform tasks and try to identify Impostors.

Customize
Computer laptop in Lobby or Freeplay start point. Allows players to change their look and edit tasks.

Discussion
Chat period allowing players to exchange information on which player might be an Impostor.

Doorlog
Ability only found in MIRA HQ. Allows players to see who has passed through security doors.

Eject
Players who have been voted out of the game are ejected and become Ghosts.

Emergency Meeting
Called when players report a dead body or the Emergency Meeting Button is pressed.

Ghost
Players who are killed come back as Ghosts and can still perform tasks or sabotage.

Hats
Cosmetic worn by character. Some hats are free, while others are purchased via the in-game store.

Impostor
One of two player roles. Impostors have to stealthily sabotage the level and kill Crewmates.

Kick
Players can be kicked out and banned from games by the host and other players in Discussions.

Kill
Impostor ability. Can only be performed when a player is close enough to a Crewmate.

Map
Screen that shows players their location, as well as the location of rooms and tasks in each level.

Mira HQ
Second map in the game. The level is in a facility high up in the Earth's atmosphere.

Pets
Cosmetic that accompanies a character, but has no function. Includes aliens, robots and UFOs.

Polus
Third map in the game. Takes place in a planetary base located on the alien world of Polus.

Report
If players discover a dead body or suspicious activity, they can report it to others in a Discussion.

Sabotage
Tasks carried out by an Impostor in a level to cause temporary mayhem for Crewmates.

Security
Room in The Skeld and Polus where players can use cameras to see where other players are.

The Skeld
First map in the game. Set on board a ship travelling through deep space.

Skins
Cosmetic worn by character. Free and paid-for skins allow players to change their appearance.

Statistics
List of the number of times a player has performed a certain task, such as quitting the game.

Tasks
One of the main Crewmate objectives. If all Tasks are completed, Crewmates win the game.

Use
Ability for players to interact with items such as Customize, Doorlog, Security and tasks.

Vent
Small hatches located in each level that allow Impostors to travel in secret from room to room.

Vision
The distance around a player that they can see clearly. Can be changed by the host at the start.

Vitals
Ability located on Polus. Allows players to check other character's vital signs and see if they're alive.

Voting
Following a Discussion, players get to decide who they think the Impostor might be and vote them out.

Online Safety Information

YOUNGER FANS' GUIDE

Spending time online with others is great fun. As Among Us might be your first experience of digital socialising, here are a few simple rules to help you stay safe and keep the internet an awesome place to spend time:

- Never give out your real name – don't use it as your username.
- Never give out any of your personal details.
- Never tell anybody which school you go to or how old you are.
- Before playing Among Us, ask a parent or guardian for permission.
- Only give out your Local and Private Among Us codes to people you know.
- Take regular breaks, as well as playing with parents nearby, or in shared family rooms.
- Always tell a parent or guardian if something is worrying you.

NOTE: Among Us is PEGI rated 7.

PARENTS' GUIDE

Online Chat

In Among Us, there is live, unmoderated on-screen text chat between users. At the time of writing, turning off text chat isn't possible.

Reporting Players

If a player is being abusive in an online game, it's best to either ignore them or leave the game altogether and find a different one to play on. Players who host a game themselves can kick abusive players out of a session and ban them completely from re-entering the game.

Screen Time

Taking regular breaks is important. Set play sessions by using a timer.

In-Game Purchases

Among Us does offer the ability for players to make in-game purchases for items such as new skins, pets, hats and bundles, also known as Cosmetics. They're not required to play the game and they don't improve a player's performance.

PC Purchases
- The paid-for PC version of Among Us includes all hats and skins for free, apart from the items included in additional bundle purchases via Steam. For PC users, go into the account settings of your child's Steam account. Once in there, make sure there aren't any card details or linked PayPal accounts. You can easily remove them if they are there.

Mobile Purchases
- On Android and iOS devices, players can purchase additional Cosmetics. For iPhone and iPad, whenever you make a purchase, you'll always have to verify it with either a password, the Touch ID fingerprint scanner or Face ID. But some iPhones are set up so that you only have to enter a password every 15 minutes. To stop this, go to Settings > Your Name > iTunes & App Store. Underneath you'll see a Password Settings Section. Go to Purchases And In-App Purchases, and choose Always Require. If your child knows your iPhone password, you can set up a second PIN for purchases. Go to Settings > General > Restrictions, then press Enable Restrictions. You can then choose a new four-digit passcode for In-App Purchases.

Nintendo Switch Purchases
- A number of hats are included for free with the Nintendo Switch version of the game. No other items are currently available for purchase on this version of the game.